PET FISH

by Robin Nelson

first step nonfiction

Lerner Publications Company · Minneapolis

A fish is an **animal.**

Fish make good **pets.**

There are many different
kinds of pet fish.

Fish live in water.

Some fish live in cold water.

Some fish live in warm water.

Pet fish can live in a bowl.

Pet fish can live in a tank
called an **aquarium.**

Fish like to **hide.**

Plants and rocks make
good hiding places.

Pet fish need food
every day.

Pet fish need a small
bit of food.

Pet fish need clean water.

Pet fish need a clean bowl.

We like to watch our fish.

We like taking care of fish.

Parts of a Fish

Fish are very good swimmers. Fish have tails and fins to help them swim. Fish have scales all over their body. These scales let the fish slide through the water. Scales also help protect the fish.

Fish use gills to breathe underwater. Fish open their mouths to let in water. The water flows over the gills. The gills take oxygen out of the water. The rest of the water flows out through the gills.

mouth

gills

fin

fin

fin

scales

fin

fin

tail

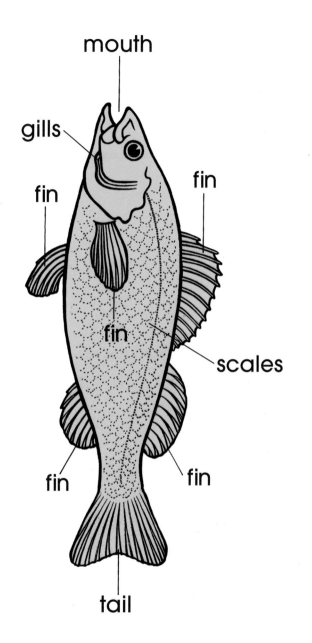

Fun Fish Facts

 Fish do not sleep. Fish rest by moving very slowly.

 Fish do not have eyelids. Their eyes are always open.

 Fish tell each other how they feel by changing the way they look or smell or by acting a special way.

 Some fish hide from enemies by digging a hole in the sand and hiding in it.

Fish are cold-blooded. This means that their bodies stay the same temperature as the water around them.

 Fish have slime all over their bodies. This slime protects them from getting sick.

Glossary

 animal – anything alive that is not a plant

 aquarium – a glass box that is filled with water

 hide – to go where nobody can see you

 pets – animals that live with people

Index

The photographs in this book are reproduced through the courtesy of: © PhotoDisc Royalty-Free Images, cover, pp. 2, 6, 22 (top); Todd Strand/Independent Picture Service, pp. 3, 7, 8, 9, 10, 11, 12, 13, 14, 15, 17, 22 (second from top, second from bottom, bottom); © Carl & Ann Purcell/CORBIS, p. 4; © Doug Wilson/CORBIS, p. 5; © Michael Pole/CORBIS, p. 16.

Illustration on page 19 by Laura Westlund.

Lerner Publications Company
A division of Lerner Publishing Group
241 First Avenue North
Minneapolis, MN 55401 USA

Website address: www.lernerbooks.com

Library of Congress Cataloging-in-Publication Data

Nelson, Robin, 1971–
        Pet fish / by Robin Nelson.
            p.   cm. — (First step nonfiction)
        Summary: A simple introduction to pet fish and their basic needs.
        ISBN: 0–8225–1267–X (lib. bdg. : alk. paper)
        1. Ornamental fishes—Juvenile literature. 2. Ornamental
fishes—Miscellanea—Juvenile literature. [1. Aquarium fishes.
2. Fishes. 3. Pets.] I. Title. II. Series.
SF457.25.N46 2003
639.34—dc21   2001006018

Manufactured in the United States of America
1 2 3 4 5 6 – AM – 08 07 06 05 04 03